Gulls

GEORGE K. PECK

SMART APPLE MEDIA

Published by

Smart Apple Media

123 South Broad Street

Mankato, Minnesota 56001

🪭

Copyright © 1998 Smart Apple Media.

International copyrights reserved in all countries.

No part of this book may be reproduced in any form without

written permission from the publisher.

Printed in the United States of America.

Photos by George K. Peck,

Mark Peck,

Steve Warble / Hillstrom Stock Photo, Inc.

Editorial assistance by Barbara Ciletti

Library of Congress Cataloging-in-Publication Data

Peck, George K.

Gulls / written by George Peck.

p. cm.

Includes index.

Summary: Describes the life cycle, behavior patterns, and habitat

of various species of gulls, focusing on those found in North America.

ISBN 1-887068-13-9

1. Gulls—Juvenile literature.   2. Gulls—North America—Juvenile literature.

[1. Gulls.]   I. Title.

QL696.C46P435   1998   96-8376

598.3'38—dc20   CIP

                                                              AC

First Edition   5 4 3 2 1

C O N T E N T S

In Salt Lake City, Utah, there stands a tall bronze monument to a savior of the Mormon people. But the statue is not of a soldier, a saint, or a politician. It is a statue of a California Gull.

In the summer of 1848, shortly after the Mormons settled the Salt Lake Valley, millions of Mormon Crickets began to devour the crops. Things looked bad for the settlers. Without their corn and wheat crops, they might not survive the coming winter.

Then the gulls came.

Thousands upon thousands of hungry California Gulls swept into the valley, eating their fill of crickets. Most of the damage had been done, but some of the crops were saved. When winter came, the Mormons had just enough food to survive. A statue was built to honor the California gull.

Today, the California Gull is the state bird of Utah.

Gulls are part of a large group of waterbirds that are found on and near oceans, lakes, and rivers. Wherever open water appears on the surface of our planet, you are likely to find gulls or their close relatives, the terns. Auks, skimmers, skuas, jaegers, and many small shorebirds such as sandpipers and plovers are also related to gulls. There are 51 species of gulls in our world. Eighteen species are known to live and breed in the United States and Canada.

Because gulls are so common in coastal areas, they are often called "sea gulls," but gulls are also found inland on lakes, rivers, and ponds.

The Franklin's Gull breeds in the prairie marshes of Alberta, Saskatchewan, and Manitoba. In the winter, it migrates to coastal areas of Central and South America. Bonaparte's Gull prefers ponds in the northern forests of Alaska and Canada, and it winters on both the Atlantic and Pacific coasts and on the Great Lakes.

Iceland Gulls gather in colonies on island cliff ledges in the far north, like those of Iceland, Greenland, and Baffin Island. They winter in North America along the Atlantic coast from Newfoundland all the way down to Virginia. The most northern species of all is the Ivory Gull, a pure white gull that is rarely seen below the Arctic Circle—not even during the winter! Colonies of Ivory Gulls nest on the northernmost islands, where snow and ice stay on the ground all year long.

The Herring Gull, one of North America's most common gulls, nests singly and in colonies all across Canada and the northern United States. It also nests on the Atlantic coast down to South Carolina, near both freshwater and saltwater. The equally common Ring-billed Gull nests in large colonies on islands and the shores of freshwater lakes and rivers, from Newfoundland in the east to Washington and Oregon in the west. Ring-billed Gulls spend their winters in the southern United States and Mexico.

Wherever there is open water, you will find gulls. They avoid only the driest, hottest deserts and the coldest parts of the Polar regions.

Gulls vary in size from the Great Black-backed Gull (about the size of a small goose), to the Little Gull (about the size of a pigeon), but all have some features in common.

Gulls are scavengers. They eat what they can find, wherever they find it, and their bodies are perfectly adapted to their lifestyle. They spend much of their time in the air, scanning the shoreline for a dead fish, a scrap of bread, or anything else that looks tasty. Their long narrow wings are perfect for spending long hours in the air. And when a gull does find food, its long bill with its hooked tip is strong and sharp enough to tear into almost anything— whether it be slippery, flopping fish, or a stolen bag of potato chips!

When gulls are not flying, they are either walking or swimming, and their long legs and webbed toes are built to do both. Dense, compact feathers keep gulls warm and dry, even when they are swimming in the coldest water.

The gull's ability to adapt to different environments and diets has made it one of the most successful and widespread bird families. They are one of the few warm-blooded animals able to drink both salt and fresh water. A pair of glands above their eyes helps get rid of the extra salt in their bodies.

Most adult gulls have gray backs and white undersides, and yellow, red, or black bills. Gull legs and feet are often yellow, but can also be red, pink, or black. Some species, like the Herring Gull and the Ring-billed Gull, can be hard to tell apart, but if you look closely, you can see a ring of black around the bill of the adult Ring-billed Gull. The adult Herring Gull has a small red spot on the bottom of its yellow bill.

Several gull species, such as the Great Black-backed Gull, have backs that are black or very dark gray. Some smaller species have black heads. The Ivory Gull of the far north is pure white. Heerman's Gull, which is found along the Pacific coast, is dark gray with a white head and a red bill.

Young gulls can be difficult to identify. Most one- and two-year-old gulls do not look like their parents. They are a mix of neutral shades of light, medium, and dark brown. Smaller gulls come into their adult plumage in their second year, but the bigger Herring Gull takes four years to become an adult—every year it looks different!

Even experts have trouble identifying young gulls—sometimes, you just have to wait for them to grow up.

A Ring-billed Gull and its colony.

Gulls eat just about anything. They clean up dead fish, crabs, and clams from harbors and beaches. They also eat live fish and prey on the eggs and young of other birds. Instead of diving deep underwater for food the way loons and penguins do, a gull will pick its catch off the water's surface.

In farming areas, flocks of gulls will follow the plows, feeding on the earthworms, grasshoppers, and other creatures disturbed by the plow blades.

Gulls also like people food, and will often gather near restaurants, picnic areas, and dumps. Almost anything will do—meat scraps, bread crusts, french fries, and chicken bones—for gulls, "junk food" is the best! The small gulls known as Black- and Red-legged Kittiwakes will follow ships far out to sea, waiting for food to be thrown overboard.

Some gulls can be very aggressive when it comes to eating. They steal food from other birds, especially the slow-moving Brown Pelican. Gulls steal from each other too. They will even snatch a treat from your picnic table.

Many beaches have signs that say, "Don't feed the gulls." This is because once you start feeding the gulls, the gulls won't leave you alone! Imagine being followed all day long by dozens of screeching, hungry birds!

In the fall, some gull species leave their northern breeding areas and head for warmer waters.   Gulls that breed in northern inland areas must travel south, or to the ocean, where the water will not freeze.

Most gulls don't go any farther than they have to. The Ivory Gull stays at the edge of the Arctic ice pack. The Herring Gull flies to the nearest open water. Many coastal gulls remain in the same area all year long. The Franklin's Gull is one of the few gulls that migrates long distances—from Canada all the way to the tip of South America.

Gulls are strong, slow flyers with an average flight speed of 25 miles per hour (40 kph), but they can soar for days at a time, setting their long, narrow wings and letting the wind do the work. Gulls often face into the wind and simply hover as if by magic, looking down at the ocean surface and waiting for dinner to appear.

Laughing Gulls in flight on the coast of Padre Island, Texas.

Gulls live together in groups, or flocks. Most gulls also nest together in large groups called colonies. A few species, such as Bonaparte's and Sabine's Gulls, sometimes nest alone.

In North America, gulls arrive at their breeding grounds in the spring, after the snows have thawed. Breeding grounds are often islands or protected shorelines where the birds will not be disturbed. Kittiwakes and Iceland Gulls nest on high sea cliffs.

Tens of thousands of gulls might share a breeding territory, sometimes sharing it with other bird species such as pelicans, herons, and terns.

Gulls begin to court one another right after arrival. Both the male and female strut back and forth, making loud mewling and yodeling sounds—*ke-yow, ke-yow, ke-yow*! With thousands of gulls all calling and strutting about, trying to get one another's attention, the noise is incredible! Fights break out between competing males. Often, the male gull will offer the female food.

Somehow, in all the confusion, the gulls work things out. Mates from previous years find one another. Young males and females form new pairs. Once a bond is formed, a pair of gulls will often remain mates for life. They may go their separate ways in the winter, but each spring they will find one another and raise a new family.

The female gull chooses the nest site. In crowded colonies, the nests might be so close to each other that you would have trouble walking through them without stepping on one! If you did that, the gulls would create quite a ruckus. Gulls are very aggressive about defending their nests.

Most gulls place their nests on the bare ground, in grasses, on rocks, or on cliff ledges. Nests are usually mounds of grasses, weeds, sticks, or mosses. They may be lined with feathers.

Not all gulls nest on the ground. The Bonaparte's Gull builds its nest on a branch of a spruce tree. The Laughing and Little Gulls nest in marshes on floating mats of dead reeds. The Black-legged Kittiwake builds its cup-shaped nest on the narrow ledges of high cliffs. It is made of seaweed, grass, moss, and mud.

Females usually lay three eggs. Kittiwakes and the Ivory Gull usually lay only two. Some gull nests have been found with five or more eggs, but this is usually because more than one female gull has laid eggs in it. Gull eggs are often brown or gray with spots and splotches of darker gray, brown, or black. Franklin's Gull lays eggs of olive green, with dark brown spots. The mother Herring Gull lays eggs that are sometimes bluish and sometimes somewhat green or buff, speckled with brown.

After the eggs are laid, the parents take turns incubating them. The eggs must be kept warm so that the embryos can develop, and they must be protected from predators, including other gulls.

The babies hatch from their eggs after three to four weeks of incubation. The smaller Franklin's Gull comes out of its shell just after three weeks, whereas California Gull babies don't hatch for nearly a month. Gull babies come into the world covered with soft down, their eyes already open. In a colony, most of the baby gulls hatch within a few days of one another. Since hungry baby gulls demand constant attention, it's an exciting time in the colony!

Baby gulls are fed and protected by both parents. The adult gulls store food in their crops, which are pouches located in their throats. The young Herring Gulls peck at the red dot on their parents' bills. This is a signal for the adult gull to bring up some partially digested food from its crop. Several other gull species have similar red dots on their bills.

In a colony with thousands of nests that all look the same, you might wonder how a parent gull can find its own nest. Gulls' colonies do not have street names. They don't have numbers on their nests. Gull parents find their own young by listening for their cries. Every baby has a voice all its own. When it cries out, its parent knows who it is.

Young Herring Gulls leave the nest within two or three days, but they don't wander far. For several weeks they depend on their parents to bring them food. It takes five or six weeks for their flight feathers to grow. Until then, the young gulls remain near the nest. If a colony is disturbed, the young gulls will run to the water and swim until the danger has passed. Kittiwakes are born on the narrow ledges of high sea cliffs. Once they jump off that ledge, there will be no second chance, so young kittiwakes stay in their nests until they are ready to fly.

Once young gulls can fly, they learn to feed themselves. They continue to beg for food from their parents, but after a while they are on their own.

As summer turns to fall, the young birds go off on their own or with other young gulls their own age. Many won't be full adults until they're three or four years old. When they're all grown up, they return to the breeding grounds where they hatched. Here, they'll find mates and raise families of their own. They may breed at this same colony for the rest of their lives.

D A N G E R S

Gulls face many dangers at their nesting colonies. The eggs and young gulls are eaten by many different predators including foxes, raccoons, hawks, and owls. Skuas and jaegers, close relatives of the gulls, also take many eggs and young. In mixed colonies, even other gulls will steal eggs and young from unprotected nests.

About half of all gull chicks die before their first birthday. Not many gulls live to be more than ten years old, but one captive Herring is known to have lived to the ripe old age of 49.

Human beings sometimes disturb gulls by visiting their nesting sites. The gulls are upset by people walking near their nests. They may refuse to take care of their eggs or their babies once a colony has been invaded by human visitors. Human pollution also kills many gulls. Oil spills can completely destroy nesting colonies. Poisons in our lakes, rivers, and oceans eventually find their way into the stomachs of gulls and other waterbirds.

Some people don't like gulls.

They think gulls are noisy and aggressive and messy.

But imagine the seashore without the gulls. What do you see?

A silent beach covered with dead fish and garbage.

Gulls are terrific scavengers. They are partly responsible for keeping our beaches and oceans clean. And for those of us who take the time to watch their soaring flight and their unique behaviors, they are one of the most fascinating bird groups. From the common Herring Gull, to the ghostly Ivory Gull of the far north, they all play a part in this natural world we all share.